Fla...

by Iain Gray

Lang**Syne**

PUBLISHING

WRITING *to* REMEMBER

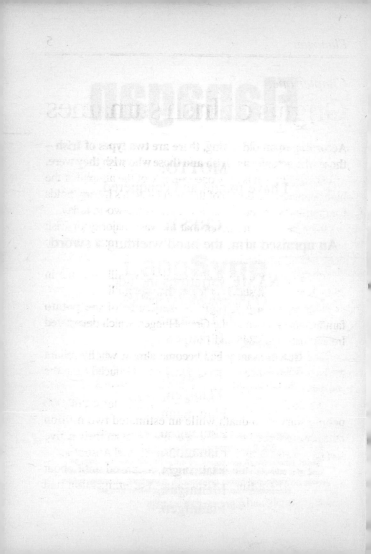

Chapter one:
Origins of Irish surnames

**According to an old saying, there are two types of Irish –
those who actually are Irish and those who wish they were.**

This sentiment is only one example of the allure that the
high romance and drama of the proud nation's history holds
for thousands of people scattered across the world today.

It's a sad fact, however, that the vast majority of Irish
surnames are found far beyond Irish shores, rather than on
the Emerald Isle itself.

The population stood at around eight million souls in
1841, but today it stands at fewer than six million.

This is mainly a tragic consequence of the potato
famine, also known as the Great Hunger, which devastated
Ireland between 1845 and 1849.

The Irish peasantry had become almost wholly reliant
for basic sustenance on the potato, first introduced from the
Americas in the seventeenth century.

When the crop was hit by a blight, at least 800,000
people starved to death while an estimated two million
others were forced to seek a new life far from their native
shores – particularly in America, Canada, and Australia.

The effects of the potato blight continued until about
1851, by which time a firm pattern of emigration had
become established.

Ireland's loss, however, was to the gain of the countries in which the immigrants settled, contributing enormously, as their descendants do today, to the well being of the nations in which their forefathers settled.

But those who were forced through dire circumstance to establish a new life in foreign parts never forgot their roots, or the proud heritage and traditions of the land that gave them birth.

Nor do their descendants.

It is a heritage that is inextricably bound up in the colourful variety of Irish names themselves – and the origin and history of these names forms an integral part of the vibrant drama that is the nation's history, one of both glorious fortune and tragic misfortune.

This history is well documented, and one of the most important and fascinating of the earliest sources are *The Annals of the Four Masters*, compiled between 1632 and 1636 by four friars at the Franciscan Monastery in County Donegal.

Compiled from earlier sources, and purporting to go back to the Biblical Deluge, much of the material takes in the mythological origins and history of Ireland and the Irish.

This includes tales of successive waves of invaders and settlers such as the Fomorians, the Partholonians, the Nemedians, the Fir Bolgs, the Tuatha De Danann, and the Laigain.

Of particular interest are the *Milesian Genealogies*,

because the majority of Irish clans today claim a descent from either Heremon, Ir, or Heber – three of the sons of Milesius, a king of what is now modern day Spain.

These sons invaded Ireland in the second millennium B.C, apparently in fulfilment of a mysterious prophecy received by their father.

This Milesian lineage is said to have ruled Ireland for nearly 3,000 years, until the island came under the sway of England's King Henry II in 1171 following what is known as the Cambro-Norman invasion.

This is an important date not only in Irish history in general, but for the effect the invasion subsequently had for Irish surnames.

'Cambro' comes from the Welsh, and 'Cambro-Norman' describes those Welsh knights of Norman origin who invaded Ireland.

But they were invaders who stayed, inter-marrying with the native Irish population and founding their own proud dynasties that bore Cambro-Norman names such as Archer, Barbour, Brannagh, Fitzgerald, Fitzgibbon, Fleming, Joyce, Plunkett, and Walsh – to name only a few.

These 'Cambro-Norman' surnames that still flourish throughout the world today form one of the three main categories in which Irish names can be placed – those of Gaelic-Irish, Cambro-Norman, and Anglo-Irish.

Previous to the Cambro-Norman invasion of the twelfth century, and throughout the earlier invasions and settlement of those wild bands of sea rovers known as the Vikings in the eighth and ninth centuries, the population of the island was relatively small, and it was normal for a person to be identified through the use of only a forename.

But as population gradually increased and there were many more people with the same forename, surnames were adopted to distinguish one person, or one community, from another.

Individuals identified themselves with their own particular tribe, or 'tuath', and this tribe – that also became known as a clann, or clan – took its name from some distinguished ancestor who had founded the clan.

The Gaelic-Irish form of the name Kelly, for example, is Ó Ceallaigh, or O'Kelly, indicating descent from an original 'Ceallaigh', with the 'O' denoting 'grandson of.' The name was later anglicised to Kelly.

The prefix 'Mac' or 'Mc', meanwhile, as with the clans of the Scottish Highlands, denotes 'son of.'

Although the Irish clans had much in common with their Scottish counterparts, one important difference lies in what are known as 'septs', or branches, of the clan.

Septs of Scottish clans were groups who often bore an entirely different name from the clan name but were under the clan's protection.

In Ireland, septs were groups that shared the same name and who could be found scattered throughout the four provinces of Ulster, Leinster, Munster, and Connacht.

The 'golden age' of the Gaelic-Irish clans, infused as their veins were with the blood of Celts, pre-dates the Viking invasions of the eighth and ninth centuries and the Norman invasion of the twelfth century, and the sacred heart of the country was the Hill of Tara, near the River Boyne, in County Meath.

Known in Gaelic as 'Teamhar na Rí', or Hill of Kings, it was the royal seat of the 'Ard Rí Éireann', or High King of Ireland, to whom the petty kings, or chieftains, from the island's provinces were ultimately subordinate.

It was on the Hill of Tara, beside a stone pillar known as the Irish 'Lia Fáil', or Stone of Destiny, that the High Kings were inaugurated and, according to legend, this stone would emit a piercing screech that could be heard all over Ireland when touched by the hand of the rightful king.

The Hill of Tara is today one of the island's main tourist attractions.

Opposition to English rule over Ireland, established in the wake of the Cambro-Norman invasion, broke out frequently and the harsh solution adopted by the powerful forces of the Crown was to forcibly evict the native Irish from their lands.

These lands were then granted to Protestant colonists, or 'planters', from Britain.

Many of these colonists, ironically, came from Scotland and were the descendants of the original 'Scotti', or 'Scots', who gave their name to Scotland after migrating there in the fifth century A.D., from the north of Ireland.

Colonisation entailed harsh penal laws being imposed on the majority of the native Irish population, stripping them practically of all of their rights.

The Crown's main bastion in Ireland was Dublin and its environs, known as the Pale, and it was the dispossessed peasantry who lived outside this Pale, desperately striving to eke out a meagre living.

It was this that gave rise to the modern-day expression of someone or something being 'beyond the pale'.

Attempts were made to stamp out all aspects of the ancient Gaelic-Irish culture, to the extent that even to bear a Gaelic-Irish name was to invite discrimination.

This is why many Gaelic-Irish names were anglicised with, for example, and noted above, Ó Ceallaigh, or O'Kelly, being anglicised to Kelly.

Succeeding centuries have seen strong revivals of Gaelic-Irish consciousness, however, and this has led to many families reverting back to the original form of their name, while the language itself is frequently found on the fluent tongues of an estimated 90,000 to 145,000 of the island's population.

Ireland's turbulent history of religious and political strife is one that lasted well into the twentieth century, a landmark century that saw the partition of the island into the twenty-six counties of the independent Republic of

Ireland, or Eire, and the six counties of Northern Ireland, or Ulster.

Dublin, originally founded by Vikings, is now a vibrant and truly cosmopolitan city while the proud city of Belfast is one of the jewels in the crown of Ulster.

It was Saint Patrick who first brought the light of Christianity to Ireland in the fifth century A.D.

Interpretations of this Christian message have varied over the centuries, often leading to bitter sectarian conflict – but the many intricately sculpted Celtic Crosses found all over the island are symbolic of a unity that crosses the sectarian divide.

It is an image that fuses the 'old gods' of the Celts with Christianity.

All the signs from the early years of this new millennium indicate that sectarian strife may soon become a thing of the past – with the Irish and their many kinsfolk across the world, be they Protestant or Catholic, finding common purpose in the rich tapestry of their shared heritage.

Chapter two:

Celtic myth and legend

The name in Gaelic is Ó Flannagáin, stemming from a term indicating 'ruddy', or 'red-haired', and it was these originally red-haired Celts who for centuries contributed to the rich and colourful tapestry that is Ireland's history.

They were to be found at different locations throughout the island, including the present day southern county of Galway, but it was the northern province of Connacht that became their main stamping ground.

Along with clans that include the O'Connors, Malones, and McDermots, the Flanagans, or O'Flanagans, were of the tribe known as the Uí Briuin – indicating an illustrious descent from the celebrated Niall Noíghiallach, through his brother Brian.

Better known to posterity as the great warrior king Niall of the Nine Hostages, the dramatic life and times of this ancestor of the Flanagans are steeped in stirring myth and legend.

The youngest son of Eochaidh Mugmedon, king of Connacht, his mother died in childbirth and he was brought up by his evil stepmother Mongfhinn, who was determined that he should die.

She accordingly abandoned him naked on the Hill of

Tara, inauguration site of the Ard Rí, or High Kings, of Ireland, but a wandering bard found him and took him back to his father.

One legend is that Mongfhinn sent Niall and his four brothers – Brian, Fiachra, Ailill, and Fergus – to a renowned prophet who was also a blacksmith to determine which of them would succeed their father as Ard Rí.

The blacksmith, known as Sitchin, set the lads a task by deliberately setting fire to his forge.

Niall's brothers ran in and came out carrying the spearheads, fuel, hammers, and barrels of beer that they had rescued, but Niall staggered out clutching the heavy anvil so vital to the blacksmith's trade.

By this deed, Sitchin prophesied that Niall would be the one who would take on the glorious mantle of kingship.

Another prophetic incident occurred one day while Niall and his brothers were engaged in the hunt.

Thirsty from their efforts they encountered an ugly old woman who offered them water – but only in return for a kiss.

Three of the lads, no doubt repelled by her green teeth and scaly skin, refused. Fiachra pecked her lightly on the cheek and, by this act, she prophesied that he would one day reign at Tara – but only briefly.

The bold Niall, however, kissed her fully on the lips. The hag then demanded that he should now have full sexual intercourse with her and, undaunted, he did so.

Through this action she was suddenly transformed into a stunningly beautiful young woman known as Flaithius, or Royalty, who predicted that he would become the greatest High King of Ireland.

His stepmother later tried to poison him, but accidentally took the deadly potion herself and died.

This legend relates to what was known as the Festival of Mongfhinn, or Feis na Samhan (the Fest of Samhain), because it was on the evening of October 31, on Samhain's Eve, that the poisoning incident is reputed to have taken place.

It was believed for centuries in Ireland that, on Samhain Eve, Mongfhinn's warped and wicked spirit would roam the land in hungry search of children's souls.

The Festival, or Feast, of Samhain, is better known today as Halloween.

Niall became Ard Rí in 379 A.D. and embarked on the series of military campaigns and other daring adventures that would subsequently earn him the title of Niall of the Nine Hostages.

The nine countries and territories into which he raided and took hostages for ransom were the Irish provinces of Munster, Leinster, Connacht, and Ulster, Britain, and the territories of the Saxons, Morini, Picts, and Dalriads.

Niall's most famous hostage was a young lad known as Succat, son of Calpernius, a Romano-Briton who lived in the area of present day Milford Haven, on the Welsh coast.

Later known as Patricius, or Patrick, he became renowned as Ireland's patron saint, St. Patrick, responsible for bringing the light of Christianity to the island in the early years of the fifth century A.D.

Raiding in Gaul, in the area of Boulogne-sur-mer in present day France, Niall was ambushed and killed by one of his treacherous subjects in 405 A.D.

But his legacy survived through the royal dynasties and clans founded by his brothers and sons.

The treasure trove of early Irish history known as *The Annals of the Four Masters* provides a wealth of information concerning the Flanagans.

They record the death in 1202 of a Conn Craibhdheach O'Flanagan, with 'Craibhdheach' indicating 'Pious', while another particularly pious Flanagan was Donough O'Flanagan, the Bishop of Elphin, in Co. Roscommon, who was renowned far and wide for his generosity and who died in 1307.

As members of the Uí Briuin, the fortunes of the Flanagans were inextricably bound to those of the Clan O'Connor sept known as the Royal O'Connors – holding the honoured post of stewards to the O'Connor Kings of Connacht.

But this did not prevent occasional petty skirmishes among the clans that comprised the Uí Briuin, and with other clans.

The annals record, for example, how, in 1303: 'Dermot

O'Flanagan, Chief of Tuathratha, his two sons, and many others along with them, were slain at Bun Duibhe by some of the household of Donnell, son of Tiege O'Conor, who had pursued them to deprive them of a prey which they were carrying off from Magh-g-Cedne.'

An O'Flanagan chief is also recorded as having been slain three years later by Brian Carragh O'Hara.

But it was as hereditary stewards of the Royal O'Connors that the Flanagans stamped their indelible mark on the pages of the Emerald Isle's turbulent tale.

So closely linked are the two clans that although they have different mottos and heraldic crests, they share the same main feature on their coats of arms of a green oak tree.

Apart from their own dominance as sub-kings of the province of Connacht, the O'Connors not only acted for a time as the High Kings of Ireland as a whole, but also in effect represented the last of the ancient institution.

One of the most celebrated of these was the twelfth century Turlough Mor O'Conor, or O'Connor, while it was his son Rory and his Flanagan allies who were destined to play a formative and ultimately tragic role in one of the most important episodes in Ireland's history.

This was after Rory took over the mantle of the High Kingship following his father's death in 1156.

Chapter three:

Rebel warriors and priests

Twelfth century Ireland was far from a unified nation, split up as it was into territories ruled over by squabbling chieftains who ruled as kings in their own right – and this inter-clan rivalry worked to the advantage of the invaders.

In a series of bloody conflicts one chieftain, or king, would occasionally gain the upper hand over his rivals, and by 1156 the most powerful was Muirchertach MacLochlainn, king of the powerful O'Neills of the province of Ulster.

He was opposed by the equally powerful Rory O'Connor, but he increased his power and influence by allying himself with Dermot MacMurrough, king of Leinster.

MacLochlainn and MacMurrough were aware that the main key to the kingdom of Ireland was the thriving trading port of Dublin that had been established by invading Vikings, or Ostmen, in 852A.D.

Their combined forces took Dublin, but when MacLochlainn died the Dubliners rose up in revolt and overthrew the unpopular MacMurrough.

A triumphant O'Connor and his Flanagan kinsfolk now entered Dublin and was later inaugurated as Ard Rí, but MacMurrough was not one to humbly accept defeat.

He appealed for help from England's Henry II in unseating O'Connor, an act that was to radically affect the future course of Ireland's fortunes.

The English monarch agreed to help MacMurrough, but distanced himself from direct action by delegating his Norman subjects in Wales with the task.

These ambitious and battle-hardened barons and knights had first settled in Wales following the Norman Conquest of England in 1066 and, with an eye on rich booty, plunder, and lands, were only too eager to obey their sovereign's wishes and furnish MacMurrough with aid.

MacMurrough crossed the Irish Sea to Bristol in 1169, and rallied powerful barons such as Robert Fitzstephen and Maurice Fitzgerald to his cause, along with Gilbert de Clare, Earl of Pembroke.

The mighty Norman war machine soon moved into action, and so fierce and disciplined was their onslaught on the forces of Rory O'Connor and his allies that they re-captured Dublin, in the name of MacMurrough, and other strategically important territories.

Henry II now began to take cold feet over the venture, realising that he may have created a rival in the form of a separate Norman kingdom in Ireland.

Accordingly, he landed on the island, near Waterford, at the head of a large army in October of 1171 with the aim of curbing the power of his Cambro-Norman barons.

But protracted war between the king and his barons was

averted when they submitted to the royal will, promising homage and allegiance in return for holding the territories they had conquered in the king's name.

Henry also received the submission and homage of many of the Irish chieftains, while English dominion over the island was ratified through the Treaty of Windsor of 1175, under the terms of which Rory O'Connor, for example, was only allowed to rule territory unoccupied by the Normans in the role of a vassal of the king.

This humiliation appears to have been too much for the proud Rory to bear, for he abdicated his kingship and took himself off to monastic seclusion.

He died in 1198, the last in a line of no less than eleven O'Connor High Kings of Ireland.

Flanagans were among the ranks of the 3,000-strong force that Felim O'Connor fielded at the second battle of Athenry in 1316 – and were among the many dead that included the O'Connor chieftain himself.

Felim's battle had been waged against English colonists, as had been those of his predecessors – one of whom is recorded in the annals as having attacked the province of Leinster with his army in 1187.

The annals state: 'He burned and demolished the castle of Kildare, where not one of the English escaped, but were all suffocated, or otherwise killed.

'They carried away their accoutrements, arms, shields, coats of mail, and horses, and slew two knights.'

The island became frequently torn apart by rebellion as the power of the English Crown and waves of colonists encroached further on the native Irish way of life.

A policy of 'plantation', or settlement of loyal Protestants in Ireland had been started during the reign from 1491 to 1547 of Henry VIII, whose Reformation effectively outlawed the established Roman Catholic faith throughout his dominions.

In an insurrection that exploded in 1641, at least 2,000 Protestant settlers were massacred at the hands of Catholic landowners and their kinsfolk, while thousands more were driven from the lands they had acquired.

Terrible as the atrocities were against the Protestant settlers, subsequent accounts became greatly exaggerated, serving to fuel a burning desire on the part of Protestants for revenge against the rebels.

The English Civil War intervened to prevent immediate action, but following the execution of Charles I in 1649 and the consolidation of the power of England's Oliver Cromwell, the time was ripe was revenge.

The Lord Protector, as he was named, descended on Ireland at the head of a 20,000-strong army that landed at Ringford, near Dublin, in August of 1649, and the consequences of this Cromwellian conquest still resonate throughout the island today.

He had three main aims: to quash all forms of rebellion, to 'remove' all Catholic landowners who had taken part in the rebellion, and to convert the native Irish to the Protestant faith.

An early warning of the terrors that were in store for the native Catholic Irish came when the town of Drogheda was stormed and taken in September and between 2,000 and 4,000 of its inhabitants killed, including priests who were summarily put to the sword.

Cromwell soon held the land in a grip of iron, allowing him to implement what amounted to a policy of ethnic cleansing, while an edict was issued stating that any native Irish found east of the River Shannon after May 1, 1654 faced either summary execution or transportation to the West Indies.

What proved to be the final death knell of families such as the Flanagans was sounded in 1688 following what was known as the Glorious Revolution.

This involved the flight into exile of the Catholic monarch James II (James VII of Scotland) and the accession to the throne of the Protestant William of Orange and his wife Mary.

Followers of James were known as Jacobites, and the Flanagans were prominent among those Jacobites who took up the sword in defence of not only the Stuart monarchy but also their religion.

In what is known as the War of the Two Kings, or the Williamite War, Ireland became the battleground for the attempt by Jacobites to restore James to his throne.

Key events from this period are still marked annually with marches and celebrations in Northern Ireland – most notably the lifting of the siege of Derry, or Londonderry, by Williamite forces in 1689 and the Williamite victory at the battle of the Boyne the following year.

The Jacobite defeat was finally ratified through the signing of the Treaty of Limerick in 1691.

An Act of Union between the British and Irish parliaments was passed in 1800, and numerous movements sprang up throughout Ireland to battle for its repeal and the restoration of Irish independence.

Prominent among these Irish Republicans was Miceal Ó Flanagáin, or Michael O'Flanagan, the Roman Catholic priest who was born in 1876 near Castlerea, in Co. Roscommon.

Ordained a priest for the diocese of Elphin in 1900 after studying for the priesthood at St. Patrick's College, in Maynooth, he became known as The Rebel Priest.

It was his firm conviction that Ireland's traditional rural economy, the Gaelic-Irish language, and the church itself were vital components in the struggle for independence, and it was a combination of these factors that led him in June of 1915 to playing the leading role in what became known as the infamous Cloonerco Bog Fight.

Curate of the parish of Ahamlish and priest of the village of Cliffoney at the time, he had organised his parishioners in their battle to retain their rights, against the claims of landowners, to cut their own peat for fuel.

Father Flanagan defied authority by cutting the first sods at the Cloonerco Bog – his rebellious stance leading to him being transferred by his bishop to another parish.

As vice-president of the Republican movement Sinn Féin, he had the honour of leading the prayers at the first meeting of the new Irish parliament, Dáil Éireann, in January of 1919.

President of Sinn Féin from 1933 to 1935, he died in 1942 and is interred in Dublin's Glasnevin Cemetery.

Chapter four:

On the world stage

Bearers of the Flanagan name have flourished in a wide variety of endeavours, not least in the world of entertainment.

Born Chaim Reuben Weintrop in 1896 in the Whitechapel district of London, **Bud Flanagan** was the popular British entertainer who took his stage name from a sergeant major he served under during the First World War.

But it was as 'Fargo, the Boy Wizard', that he made his stage debut at the age of 12, performing conjuring tricks.

He teamed up in 1919 with Chesney Allen to form the comedy double act Flanagan and Allen, a relationship that lasted until Allen's retirement from show business in 1945.

Starting as music hall comedians the duo later became successful recoding and film stars, recording famous songs of the Second World War era such as *We're Going to Hang Out the Washing on the Siegfried Line* and *Underneath the Arches*.

In later years Flanagan enjoyed a resurgence in his popularity with *Who Do You Think You Are Kidding Mr. Hitler* – the signature song for the British sitcom *Dad's Army* that he recorded shortly before his death in 1968.

In contemporary times **Tommy Flanagan**, born in 1965

in Glasgow, is the Scottish actor whose many screen credits include *Braveheart*, *Face Off*, *Gladiator*, *Aliens v Predator*, and the television mini-series *Attila*.

Born in 1989 in Bolton, Lancashire, **Helen Flanagan** is the English actress who is best known for her role as Rosie Webster in the British soap *Coronation Street*, while **Hallie Flanagan**, born in 1889 in Redfield, South Dakota, and who died in 1969, was the multi-talented American theatrical producer and director, author, and playwright whose life story was chronicled in the 1999 movie *Cradle Will Rock*.

Responsible for setting up the Federal Theatre Project during the Great Depression of the 1930s, she is recognised as having helped to bring theatre to ordinary Americans who had never previously experienced it.

Born in 1941 in Dublin **Fionnuala Flanagan** is the award-winning Irish actress whose film roles include the 2001 *The Others*, the 2005 *Transamerica*, and the 2007 *Paddywhackers*, while **Pauline Flanagan** was the Irish stage actress born in Co. Sligo in 1925.

The actress, who died in 2003, won an Olivier Award two years before her death for her outstanding performance in *Dolly West's Kitchen*.

Born in Los Angeles in 1967, **Joe Flanagan** is the American actor best known for his role as John Sheppard in the *Stargate Atlantis* television series, while **Crista Flanagan**, born in Mount Vernon, Illinois, in 1976, is the

American television and stand-up comedian who appeared in the 2007 *Epic Movie*.

In the world of music **Thomas Lee Flanagan** was the American jazz pianist who was nominated for four Grammy awards over the course of his career.

Born in 1930 in Detroit the musician, who died in 2001, was an accompanist of Ella Fitzgerald and also played on a number of famous recordings that include Sonny Rollins' *Saxophone Colossus* and John Coltrane's *Giant Steps*.

Flanagans have also excelled in the highly competitive world of sport.

Born in 1873 in Kilbreedy, Co. Limerick and immigrating to America when he was aged 24, **John Jesus Flanagan** was the Irish-American athlete who won three gold Olympic medals for the hammer throw – in 1900, 1904, and 1908.

The athlete, who returned to settle in his native Ireland in 1924, died in 1938.

Another noted athlete of Irish stock was **Kevin O'Flanagan**, born in Dublin in 1919 and who died in 2006.

Not only a sportsman but also a medical doctor and a sports administrator, he was a champion sprinter, long jumper, and football and rugby player.

In 1946 he famously played rugby for Ireland against France – playing football a mere seven days later for his nation against Scotland.

Serving on the International Olympic Committee from

1976 to 1994, he was later made an honorary lifetime member of the body.

On the golf course **Nick Flanagan** is the leading Australian golfer who was born in 1984 in Belmont, New South Wales.

Winner of the 2003 U.S. Amateur, making him the first non-American winner since 1971, he turned professional a year later and, at the time of writing, plays on the PGA Tour.

On the cycling circuit **Paddy Flanagan**, born in 1941 in Kildangan, Co. Kildare, was a top Irish cyclist of the 1960s and 1970s and a winner on two occasions of the island's gruelling race known as the Rás Tailtean.

Mixing the world of sport with the equally competitive world of politics **Séan Flanagan**, born in 1922 in Aughnamore, Co. Mayo, and who died in 1993, was the Gaelic footballer and Fianna Fáil party politician who served as the Republic's Minister for Health from 1966 to 1969 and as Minister for Lands from 1969 to 1973.

As a Gaelic footballer he played for Mayo and captained the All-Ireland final winning sides of 1950 and 1951.

The Gaelic Athletic Association posthumously honoured him in 2000 by naming him on its Gaelic Football Team of the Millennium.

Born in 1920 **Oliver J. Flanagan** was the Irish Fine Gael party politician who served in the Irish Parliament, Dáil Éireann, for 43 years, serving as father of the Dáil from

1981 until his retirement from politics in 1987, the same year as his death.

A social conservative, he once memorably declared that 'there was no sex in Ireland before television.'

In American politics **James Wainwright Flanagan**, born in 1805 in Virginia, was the farmer, merchant, and lawyer who served as Lieutenant-Governor of Texas in 1869 and 1870 and who represented the state in the U.S. Senate from 1870 to 1875.

Born in Derry, Northern Ireland, in 1914, **Sir James Flanagan** was the first and only Roman Catholic chief constable of the Royal Ulster Constabulary (R.U.C.), a post he held from 1973 until his retirement in 1976. He died in 1999.

Born in Belfast in 1949, **Sir Ronald Flanagan** also held the post for a time. In 2001 he became chief constable of the force's renamed successor, the Police Service of Northern Ireland (P.S.N.I.).

He resigned from the post in 2002 and, at the time of writing, serves in Her Majesty's Inspectorate of Constabulary.

In the creative world of literature **Roderick Flanagan** was the historian, writer, poet, and anthropologist who was born in 1828 in Elphin, Co. Roscommon, and later immigrated to Australia.

He is noted for his major history of New South Wales, published in the same year as his death in 1862.

Born in Tasmania in 1961 **Richard Flanagan** is the contemporary Australian historian and author whose books include the 1994 *Death of a River Guide* and the 1997 *The Sound of One Hand Clapping*.

Born in 1923 in Greenwich, Connecticut, **Thomas Flanagan** was the distinguished professor of English literature at the University of California, in Berkeley, who was the author of a series of Irish historical novels that include the 1979 *The Year of the French*.

He died in 2002.

Take a close look at the base of Washington's neck on the Washington U.S. quarter dollar coin and you will spot the initials of **John Flanagan**.

Flanagan, who was born in 1865 and died in 1952, designed the coin, first issued in 1932, and he was also the American sculptor who designed a special medallion to commemorate the First World War battle of Verdun.

In the ecclesiastical sphere **Father Edward J. Flanagan** was the priest who was born in 1886 in Leabeg, Co. Roscommon and later immigrated to America.

Ordained a priest in 1912, he became famous for founding the community for homeless boys near Omaha known as Boy's Town.

Spencer Tracy portrayed Father Flanagan, who died in 1948, in the 1938 movie *Boy's Town*.

One truly original and creative Flanagan is the American inventor Gillis Flanagan, born in 1944 in Oklahoma.

The holder of advanced degrees in an impressive range of subjects that include medicine and chemistry, he was the inventor at the age of only 14 of the Neurophone – a device that transmits sound through the skin to the brain.

The invention earned him a profile in *Life Magazine* in which he was described as a 'unique, mature, and inquisitive scientist.'

Flanagan claims that as a small child he had a recurrent dream in which he was visited by aliens who measured his intelligence by placing a silver helmet over his head.

They then told him that if his superior intelligence did not match their expectations then he and the rest of the world would be destroyed.

Key dates in Ireland's history from the first settlers to the formation of the Irish Republic:

circa 7000 B.C.	Arrival and settlement of Stone Age people.
circa 3000 B.C.	Arrival of settlers of New Stone Age period.
circa 600 B.C.	First arrival of the Celts.
200 A.D.	Establishment of Hill of Tara, Co. Meath, as seat of the High Kings.
circa 432 A.D.	Christian mission of St. Patrick.
800-920 A.D.	Invasion and subsequent settlement of Vikings.
1002 A.D.	Brian Boru recognised as High King.
1014	Brian Boru killed at battle of Clontarf.
1169-1170	Cambro-Norman invasion of the island.
1171	Henry II claims Ireland for the English Crown.
1366	Statutes of Kilkenny ban marriage between native Irish and English.
1529-1536	England's Henry VIII embarks on religious Reformation.
1536	Earl of Kildare rebels against the Crown.
1541	Henry VIII declared King of Ireland.
1558	Accession to English throne of Elizabeth I.
1565	Battle of Affane.
1569-1573	First Desmond Rebellion.
1579-1583	Second Desmond Rebellion.
1594-1603	Nine Years War.
1606	Plantation' of Scottish and English settlers.
1607	Flight of the Earls.
1632-1636	Annals of the Four Masters compiled.
1641	Rebellion over policy of plantation and other grievances.
1649	Beginning of Cromwellian conquest.
1688	Flight into exile in France of Catholic Stuart monarch James II as Protestant Prince William of Orange invited to take throne of England along with his wife, Mary.
1689	William and Mary enthroned as joint monarchs; siege of Derry.
1690	Jacobite forces of James defeated by William at battle of the Boyne (July) and Dublin taken.

1691	Athlone taken by William; Jacobite defeats follow at Aughrim, Galway, and Limerick; conflict ends with Treaty of Limerick (October) and Irish officers allowed to leave for France.
1695	Penal laws introduced to restrict rights of Catholics; banishment of Catholic clergy.
1704	Laws introduced constricting rights of Catholics in landholding and public office.
1728	Franchise removed from Catholics.
1791	Foundation of United Irishmen republican movement.
1796	French invasion force lands in Bantry Bay.
1798	Defeat of Rising in Wexford and death of United Irishmen leaders Wolfe Tone and Lord Edward Fitzgerald.
1800	Act of Union between England and Ireland.
1803	Dublin Rising under Robert Emmet.
1829	Catholics allowed to sit in Parliament.
1845-1849	The Great Hunger: thousands starve to death as potato crop fails and thousands more emigrate.
1856	Phoenix Society founded.
1858	Irish Republican Brotherhood established.
1873	Foundation of Home Rule League.
1893	Foundation of Gaelic League.
1904	Foundation of Irish Reform Association.
1913	Dublin strikes and lockout.
1916	Easter Rising in Dublin and proclamation of an Irish Republic.
1917	Irish Parliament formed after Sinn Fein election victory.
1919-1921	War between Irish Republican Army and British Army.
1922	Irish Free State founded, while six northern counties remain part of United Kingdom as Northern Ireland, or Ulster; civil war up until 1923 between rival republican groups.
1949	Foundation of Irish Republic after all remaining constitutional links with Britain are severed.